# DIGGING IN:
## How To Have Fun, Get Involved in your Community and Turn a Profit as a Plant and Garden Educator
by
**LaVera Wilson**

## Introduction

The advent of the personal computer and increasing technology has made communication easier. A woman may be in London with her child, turn on her laptop computer and send a video message to her husband in India letting him know she and the baby had a safe flight. Yes, communicating for humankind has become easier and faster. But, what of our own relationship with nature? Has all the technical progress brought us closer to our natural world? Many would answer no. Throughout the years we have become increasingly alienated from nature and society and some have begun to feel the burn. Notable Futurist and author **Faith Popcorn** suggests the "**Save Our Society**" trend will become stronger. People see the state of their communities and their planet and feel the desire to see a marked change, a change to a simpler time when people shared the harvests of their own gardens, and got closer to neighbors in their communities.

In the book *Horticulture As Therapy: Principles and Practices* by Sharon P. Simpson PhD and Martha Strauss HTM we read: "Another important step in the evolution of Horticulture therapy was initiated in 1817, when the first private psychiatric institution in the United States opened in Philadelphia. Then named the 'Asylum for Persons Deprived of their Reason,' Friends Hospital went well beyond the concept of therapy through field labor. Instead of a farm setting, Friends Hospital created a park-like setting, carefully designing into the landscape shaded walks, quiet forest paths, and open grassy meadows. Although patients still were involved in vegetable and fruit growing, this direct pursuit of the calming effects of the natural environment, as a passive form of therapy, was a new and innovative use of horticulture as a treatment tool" (Straus, 1987). Through horticulture pleasures, patients' senses were awakened and their feelings redirected, and through the peaceful and safe setting of the hospital's landscape, and environment conducive to recovery was provided. This concept was taken to another level in 1879, when Friends Hospital installed the first greenhouse solely for therapeutic purposes (Lewis, 1976). We can see that access to a green environment can benefit us. Our stress levels tend to go down as we immerse ourselves in the plant world. We can also learn about delicious and healthy foods by working in the garden and making vital connections to our fellow neighbors by working in community gardens.

For some jobs of the future may be ones that will require practical knowledge about our environment which will include focus on organic/heirloom seed growing and saving, planting with the seasons, and the way we intentionally heal ourselves with plant based herbal remedies reflecting the change of our role between people and plants. The emerging field of eco-psychology, a field which focus is to work with clients and prescribe engagements in nature, recommending walks and hikes in parks and richly wooded forests with the purpose of quiet restoration.

**"DIGGING IN: How To Have Fun, Get Involved in your Community and Turn a Profit as a Plant and Garden Educator"** is a book that in 9 steps will inspire the nature spirit within you and spark your creativity and imagination. Most importantly this book will give you 9 basic step-by-step directions on how to find work or create a business of your own that can be a wonderful addition to your community.

The information in this book is based upon the research, actual job opportunities, and experiences of the Author. The jobs mentioned in this book are by no means an exhaustive list of opportunities to work in nature. Each city and state will have it's own existing programs and the reader may experience success finding work with a nature-based organization or creating a specialized niche of their own, which is why the Author and Publisher are not

responsible for any adverse consequences resulting from

the use of any of the strategies discussed in the book.

## Table of Contents

Chapter 1      **Education**

* Junior College * Adult Education * Community Center Offerings * Local Plant and Flower Societies * Local "Urban Homesteaders" * Arboretum and Garden Workshops * Libraries * Prior Knowledge

Chapter 2      **Finding Your "Green" Niche**

* What type of Environmental Educator will you be? * School Garden Educator * Therapeutic, Healing Garden Educator * Horticulture Therapist * Biodynamic Educator * Permaculturist * Eco Therapist * Niche garden designer * Survivalist/Naturalist Educator * Urban Homesteader

Chapter 3      **Who Can I Work With, And Where Will I Work?**

* School Gardens (Elementary through High School) * Senior Centers * Community Centers * Cancer Centers * Health and Wellness Centers * Local Park and Recreation Centers * Palliative Care Centers * Hospitals and Clinics * Community Gardens * Homeschool Groups * Individuals

Chapter 4      **Crafting Your Business Plan**

* Business Planning with an Environmental Focus * Action Plan * Goal Setting * REWARD YOURSELF * Resume and Cover Letter * Independent Contracting * Licensure and Taxes * Branding Your Green Image * Contracts

Chapter 5      **Marketing**

* Word of Mouth * Flyers * Business Cards * Website * Blog * Social Media Sites * Community Partnering * Festivals, Fairs, Exhibitions

Chapter 6      **Green Your Funding Search and Maximize Your Potential Profits!**

* School District Funding for Garden Education * School Fundraisers * Friends of Local Library Branches * Grants for Health and Wellness * Senior Program Funding * Local, State and National Grants for Gardens, Environment * Associations and Leagues * Local Gardening Clubs * Local Businesses * Crowd Funding

## <u>APPENDIX</u>

* Need for young farmers, AG Dept gives/offers low interest loans * China wants food exports * Vets get Hort therapy * NY Times Patricia Leigh Brown, Feb 2011 (published) "Helping Soldiers Trade Their Swords for Plows" * Bob Woodruff Foundation – farming fellowships for wounded young vets * Veterans for sustainable agriculture * Wheelchair accessible farm * Shooting Star CSA – SF * Andrew Weil, Spontaneous Happiness * How to Solicit in kind Donantions (501c3 will have a non profit status ___ for tax write off for business)

## Chapter 1 - Education

In order to style yourself an "Environmental Educator" and get paid for your expertise, you will need to be armed with a certain amount of knowledge. The one question you will need to ask yourself is "What do I already know?" Have you gardened as a child with a parent or grandparent? (If so, those memories could be key factors in presenting and in attaining grant funding). Were you in a 4-H Club and spent time with their gardening group? If you have prior experience or knowledge, you will want to maximize it. If you have no knowledge of nature or environmental concerns you may need to get some education under your belt. Here are some options to get you the knowledge you need to start sharing your "Green Gift" with the world.

## **Junior College and Adult Schools**

Junior colleges and Adult Schools offer a wonderful variety of courses from which to choose from. Courses such as, Landscape Design, Propagation, Pruning, Tree Identification, Horticulture Therapy, Permaculture Design, Green Irrigation, Rain Water Harvesting, Fruit and Vegetable Planting, Cacti and Succulent Growing. There are a myriad of classes all across our nation that can provide information about natural systems. Often these courses can be taken as stand-alone and not as a part of a longer program. They also are considerably more affordable to participate in.

## Community and Senior Centers

Often community centers offer brief courses on gardening topics in a localized neighborhoods. Summer time is a great time when college students come to volunteer or work with neighborhood residents. Senior Centers also have program directors who organize activities for their clients, and gardening lectures workshops that sometimes last a series of weeks.

## Local Plant and Flower Societies

Local Plant and Flower Societies offer annual competitions, shows, and meetings times and appreciate sharing their love of cultivation particular plants and flowers. They are a wealth of information specific to that particular plant or flower.

## Local "Urban Homesteaders"

In Northern California there is an organization called Urban Homesteaders. The Director of this non-profit hosts workshops throughout the year on such interesting skills as Cheese-making, Mead and Beer making, Bee-keeping, Canning Jams, and raising chickens. This organization is in the thick of an urban population, yet is a micro farm. Classes here are moderately priced and helpful for connecting one with local neighbors as well as gaining skills that seem to have disappeared from modern society. Are there any in your neighborhood going "back to the land" in the city? Why not check it out?

## Arboretum and Garden Workshops

Arboretums and Garden Workshops offer excellent opportunities to hear lectures from some of the most educated naturalists. Courses such as Native Plant Gardening, Creating Natural Plant Dye Beds, Watershed Plants and Animals, Ancient Plants in Modern Societies and how we use them, and Growing Roses.

## Local Libraries

Not to be discounted are our local libraries. Your library card is a pass to as much knowledge as you can take in. Any books on Garden Design, Plants, Flowers, Sustainable Environments, and more are there. Libraries are a free resource and sometimes offer garden or plant lectures for free to the community. Other opportunities include Nature Centers and Eco-Therapy counseling.

## Chapter 2 – Finding Your Green Niche

What type of Environmental/Garden Educator would you like to be? Now that you are considering work in the natural world you will find that there are many work choices and areas in which to choose from. This chapter will cover some exciting areas in which the services of a niche garden educator may thrive.

### School Garden Educator

I saw a listing for a School Garden Educator in California. The position was full-time and salaried with benefits. As most schools operate between 8 to 9 months of the year, the educator would only work when school was in session. School gardens have now become part of school curriculum; they are able to support science, math, social studies, and art for students year round. Full integration of a garden curriculum for students enables a hands-on learning process. Advances in information linking involvement with nature and health has helped to inspire integrated programming within schools, so now administrative staff and principles are able to access grants and set aside money within their budgets for garden educator positions. In order to work at a school you will need appropriate vaccinations to work with youth. Also, experience teaching or working with children is highly encouraged. You will need to know the age level you would like to work with as you may be excited about helping first graders plant seeds and pull up carrots, but turned-off by the challenge to get teenagers to work in the soil.

## Healing Garden Educator (Therapeutic Landscape Design)

Healing gardens are relaxing. They are designed specifically with contemplative and peaceful design elements. Individuals that design gardens with a healing theme as it's focus pay particular attention to pathways and plant textures that are pleasing to the eye, seating areas for restful meditation, and unhurried areas from which to reflect. A Zen style Japanese garden with its precisely manicured miniature trees and fine sand pathways would be a good example of a contemplative space.

## Horticultural Therapist

A horticultural therapist is someone who works with people and plants to promote health and well-being. As a horticultural therapist, I have been able to work with individuals from a variety of backgrounds and come together for the common theme of caring for plants. I have enjoyed working with young children and seniors as well people with cerebral palsy. Plants do not judge. Your care of your plants or your garden space depends on the attentiveness and loving kindness for something other than oneself. A horticulture therapist works to support a client's healing process by working with plants. They work in hospitals and clinics as part of a medical team. They work in jails and with at risk youth. A very interesting clientele I have been able to work with are Alzheimer's patients.

## Biodynamic Educators

Biodynamics is the holistic view of the interrelationships between the soil, plants, animals, planet elements, man, and spirituality. Biodynamic gardening or farming is quite labor intensive, focusing on no waste and using purely organic methods of growing and harvesting. People have noticed the difference in the taste of biodynamic wines over conventionally grown wines. This version of gardening relies on all forms of life, insects, weeds and even cow horns which serve as containers for compost (which will become a concentrated liquid tincture for your garden). Biodynamics was pioneered by Rudolf Steiner. In order to teach these principles you will need to find the nearest Biodynamic farm or garden.

## Permaculturist

Someone who practices the principles of Permaculture works hard to create substantial living spaces that follow the patterns found in nature. Permaculture is a wonderful design concept built on zero waste, recycling, having your food garden close to your living space, and your animals living around that space. Particular attention is paid to the outer "wild" areas which allow for exploration and growth. The principles for permaculture are based on thousands of years of indigenous techniques. Another important aspect is green buildings, using natural materials from your surroundings in the process of making a home. In order to teach about permaculture, search online regarding permaculture, and you are bound to find an almost endless amount of information. Who knows, you might travel all over the world teaching and building!

## Ecotherapist

Eco Therapy is a combination of Ecology and Therapy. In our busy modern times people have anxiety and stress about what is happening to our planet. Things such as: global warming, oil spills, and deforestation, which effects our dynamic breathing ecosystem. Mental health professionals have taken up the reins in order to help individuals deal with their stress related worry about our planet, so we now have Eco Therapists who help people to slow down and reconnect with nature. Some therapists have taken their practice outdoors, and they prescribe walks and bird watching for their clients. To become an Eco Therapist you will need to have a license to practice therapy. Then you would pursue further training specific to nature-based therapy and connecting humans with the natural world for healing.

## Niche Garden Designer

Do you have gardens that you gravitate to? Succulents and cacti, butterfly hummingbird or maybe Californian or Mediterranean natives? As a niche garden designer, you can let your imagination run wild with ideas for plantings. With you and your client at the helm you could make their dreams come true. Apartment dwellers need not be left out. They can have small, raised-bed vegetable or herb gardens that they tend to, or beautifully crafted terrariums right in their apartments. If you are working long hours in dry office spaces, you may add interest and increase your fresh air by adding miniaturized terrariums to your desk area.

## Survivalist/Naturalist Educator

Do you have experience in leading groups on nature trails? Are you the person they look for to point out the poison oak or plants that are edible along woodsy paths? Then you may want to consider working as a nature educator for parks or community centers. In these perilous times of uncertainty, natural disasters can seemingly come from nowhere. A survival education would be a key speaker to have to educate the public on things they can do in case of a natural disaster, how to know which plants are safe to eat, where to find a water source and any other survival skills that are not really taught in schools or at home. Survival skills can be important in helping keep people calm and using our personal skills and resources to help get communities back on their feet.

# Chapter 3 – Who Can I Work With, and Where Will I Work?

## School Gardens

School Gardens (Elementary through High School) offer positions called Garden Educator. You may work with Elementary, Middle School and High School students and teachers and sometimes parents appreciate being a part of the Gardening and Environmental Education.

## Senior Centers

Senior Centers are wonderful places to work. I have participated in Horticulture Therapy programming at several centers, one of them was an assisted living center for those who have Alzheimer's. This population was able to benefit particularly because fond memories of younger years were triggered. The Activities Director is the person that should be approached about your garden program or workshop.

## Community Centers

Community Centers offer space indoors and outdoors for garden and environmental workshops to take place. Speak with the Center Director about programming.

## Cancer Centers

In Northern California there are several Cancer Centers that focus on the health of the person with cancer. I have offered massage as a Certified Massage Practitioner to women and men in various stages of cancer treatments. In the center where I worked the women also benefited from Pilates and Yoga, cooking and nutrition classes. A garden workshop might fit this group nicely. It would be important to talk to the Director about any future classes you would like to offer.

## Health and Wellness Centers

Health and Wellness Centers and Spas are places of interest that attract individuals who are concerned with their nutrition and well-being. Offering a course here would be a wonderful addition to any program that focuses on how humans interact with their natural world and how to be

a steward of the land, as well as relieve stress.

## Local Park and Recreation Centers

Local Park and Recreation Centers offer year-round

programming for young children and bingo for older adults.

Check with the Center Director about offering your

program.

## Palliative Care Centers

It is possible to work in an environment that is

considered "End Of Life." Soil-less mixes

allow people who have a measure of energy to engage in

the natural world. A therapeutic healing garden can be

designed even on the smallest level, like a terrarium that

they could look at from their bedside.

## Hospitals and Clinics

As a Horticultural Therapist in training, I was able to do

an internship with the Enid Haupt Glass Garden in

Manhattan, NY. I was impressed by the level of

professionalism that existed between physical therapy staff, doctors and patients. We were able to work with young people in the hospital with soil-less mixes. The most surprising discovery was how intent the parents and caregivers were to participate in a plant transplanting activity. Often caregivers spend many stressful hours waiting for their loved one to heal, creating a program for this population is exciting and needed.

## Community Gardens

Community Gardens are places to gather. Neighbors come to plant, grow and share. This would be an ideal place in which to teach a workshop or give a presentation about your particular Green Niche Business.

## Home-school Groups

Home-school groups are a busy bunch. Often people assume "Home-school" to mean that the families are bound to their home! Nothing is further from the truth! Homeschooling families are mobile and parents are taking their learners to classes and workshops in Spanish, History, Geometry and Art. Why not join a homeschooling group and introduce them to your business and skill in the world of nature, and how it relates to their child's education. These parents tend to have flexible schedules and workshops can often be held at someone home or a park or a local community center.

## Individuals

As a Garden/Environmental Educator you are free to work with individuals to create Healing Gardens, Butterfly Hummingbird Gardens, Edible Landscaping. The creative ideas are endless. As an Independent Contractor you can vary work with groups and with individuals.

## Chapter 4 – Crafting Your Business Plan

Business planning with an Environmental focus will allow you to fine tune your special niche. You have chosen your particular field of interest and now your task is to visualize your business up and running. There are a number of websites and books that offer templates for a small or independent business. Your job is to tailor the business plan to the niche you have chosen. Local Small Business Associations (SBA) and SCORE an organization of retired business professionals who are willing to consult with you for free are accessible in most major metropolitan cities.

## Action Plan

The most important step in your new "Green" venture is to get started. An Action Plan will help you to focus on what you should be doing and when. An action plan differs from a business plan; it is more immediate and it has specific dates when you would like to get things done. You can make a weekly or daily plan in order to keep you motivated. Try talking to at least three people a week about what you do, or a nature class you would love to teach. Visit at least two places that may be interested in your gardening workshop or environmental skills. Make a plan and check off the goals you complete.

## Goal Setting

Goal setting allows you to keep the present and the future in focus. As your nature niche becomes more clear and you knowledge and skills grow you will feel confident in achieving the goals you set forth for your green business. Your goals planning will remind you of the reason you are doing what you are doing. It will solidify the steps you need to take.

## Reward Yourself

I once took a course in which we were given lengthy homework assignments, our professor asked us to add a "reward" to our assignment. We had to do something that was purely selfish. Some people scheduled themselves a long soak in a tub, others chose a hike in the woods. This was such a helpful exercise, it allowed for reflection and self-appreciation, although it was such a challenge to "schedule" time for yourself. As you complete your own milestones on the way to building your business, treat yourself to a walk in the fresh air, a good meal or time with friends, anything that may help to relieve stress and encourage you to push ahead.

## Resume and Cover Letter

A polished resume and cover letter or letter of introduction, are key to letting people know you are out there loving the natural world and want to share that love with others. Pay particular attention to your font, format and style of your resume. I would recommend visiting your local library or checking online to find successful and working templates.

## Independent Contracting

When I was commissioned to do a project for a group of students who frequented a local library I worked as an independent contractor. If you are working solo you are considered a Sole Proprietor. You are responsible for your own taxes and insurance. The great thing is that you will be able to work on private accounts with individuals, non-profits as well as for-profit organizations.

## Licensure and Taxes

As stated above, when you work as a Sole Proprietor you are responsible for you own taxes and expenses, you may be able to write off business expenses like mileage, equipment for working garden projects, a laptop for PowerPoint presentations about your particular garden topic. You want to be sure to research all avenues that would benefit your fledgling business.

## Insurance

Your work in or around natural areas will require you to obtain some form of personal liability insurance. In case of an accident or disputes over work performed you will want to have insurance coverage.

## Branding Your Green Image

Your image is everything. Branding your particular skill set and knowledge is important to stand out. You want people to find you when they type Environmental Education Workshops or Nature Walks for Children and Seniors. Make sure your business cards and any stationary or website all have the same theme. This will make it easier for someone to connect you with your image.

## Contracts

This is the lifeblood of your business. It is vital that you have your own contracts made. You can find good books on contracts from NOLO Press. Your membership in your chosen organization may even offer contract templates for those who already freelance in the environmental field. Once you have your contract you may want to have an attorney look it over for a small fee, there are also Lawyers in the Library, a day or two that is set aside for lawyers to assist at a local library branch advising community members on their various issues. This is usually done for free, but there is often a sign-up sheet and is only offered a few times during the month. Check your local branch library.

## Chapter 5 – Marketing

### <u>Word of Mouth</u>

Word of Mouth is a simple phrase but what it generates can pay off for years to come. When someone has a positive experience learning from you at a workshop or working with you on a commissioned project, they will tell others. Someone raves about your informative workshop about how to create an efficient raised bed out of recycled materials that you have around your home, next they would like to talk after the workshop, this form of marketing may develop into privately contracted jobs as people have seen and heard good things about you.

### <u>Flyers</u>

If posted strategically, flyers can really target the audience you want to appeal to. Local bookstores, coffee shops, garden centers and libraries are all places that may post your flyer. Your flyer will need to tell who you are, your experience and your skills or services with Gardening or Environmental Education.

## Business Cards

Websites like VistaPrint offer excellent deals on business cards with a relatively low expense. A simple eye will serve you well in choosing design. In the beginning a basic but eye-catching card will get your point across. Make sure your name and your contact numbers are clear and large enough to see.

## Website

If you are tech savvy and know how to create a website I would encourage you to do so. A website can be a valuable tool. It can show your knowledge and skills, and it will allow people to read about your enthusiasm about nature. By choosing your virtual and visual elements strategically, you can draw in your audience to want to know more, avail themselves of your services or find out where you will be speaking or working next. It is also an excellent way for people to contact you with potential work.

## Blogs

If you don't already have a blog or read blogs you are in for a treat. Originally blogs began as online journals, a place where an individual could share their thoughts and photos and meanderings with a wide audience base. Blogs still serve as online journals but now they are also a means of connecting with locals and beyond. Some crafters have blogs that talk about their recent projects, workshops that they went to or have taught with photos. A blog might be a unique way to keep people posted about your thoughts and projects you may be working on or hope to be a part of. It would also be a great way to connect with others interested in the natural world. Once your passion is visible to others you will attract like individuals.

## Social Media Sites

Social media sites like Twitter, Facebook, and LinkedIn are all sites where you can connect with a large audience of people and in some cases immediately. Does someone need to attend your latest workshop at the Junior College? Is there an event to help build raised beds or create a butterfly garden? These sites may be very helpful for your business. Pinterest can be a platform to showcase particular garden design projects and provide colorful visuals that draw others in.

## Community Partnering

Sometimes people in a community partner together. Businesses and residents working together to get projects done in the neighborhood. Your services as a garden or environmental educator would be a fresh addition to a local group who would be interested in classes on seasonal nature topics for youth, or seniors or anyone interested in learning to be more self-reliant.

## Festivals, Fairs, Exhibitions

All year long each state will host a variety of festivals and country fairs. These will be excellent venues to find out who's there in the world of garden and garden design. It's also a chance to speak with people who have jobs we find

exciting and want to know more about.

# Chapter 6 – Green Your Funding Search and Maximize Your Earning Potential Profits!

## School District Funding for Garden Education

As mentioned earlier in this book, some school districts can plan within their budget. Check with your local school district job web site. Garden Educators have begun to become a part of the school budget, so it is worth approaching the school principal to find out if such a position exists or could one be created.

## School Fundraisers

Throughout the school year PTA (Parent and Teacher's Association) organizations work tirelessly to dream up fun and exciting activities for parents such as dances, bake sales, and themed parties. Parents and teachers host these activities in order to raise money for desired programming for the students. A series of after school gardening workshops would educate the children as well as teach cooperation.

## Friends of Local Libraries

The neighbors who make up the Friends of the Library have a particular focus, to support and raise money for their local library branch. Money that is raised by the "Friends" groups pay for author book signings, seasonal programming for children and the purchase of needed materials that may not be allotted for the budget.

As a Horticultural Therapist I was able to approach my local children's librarian about co-hosting an Earth Day Celebration. The children and I created signage for a raised bed garden that we built in front of the branch. This job I negotiated for free. Several weeks later, based on the tangible difference we saw in the students after completing their garden space, I approached the children's librarian once again. This time I had a copy of a series of workshops I could lead with the students after school. As many youths rely on the libraries as a safe space between leaving school and waiting on a parent or caregiver, I could provide supervision and environmental education by additional plantings in raised bed gardens behind the library. I was able to negotiate a generous fee for working with the students two days a week, for a few hours, and the Friends of the Library raised the funds. I enjoyed this series of workshops, and it was a welcome relief for librarians who could direct some of their students about the programming on site.

## Grants for Health and Wellness

There are grants for Health and Wellness that would be appropriate for Garden and Environmental Education. Nutrition Grants directly relate to Health and Wellness. With a large number of our society's population obese, it will be key to be there for work with organizations at the forefront of making great strides to reform our thinking about healthy food.

## Senior Program Funding

Senior Center facilities and Assisted Living Centers often have an Activity Director. The Activities Director is responsible for programming for the seniors at the facility. He or she may have a budget which allows them to hire musicians, artists, I would encourage you to approach the Activities Director with a series of workshops that you could provide to the seniors.

Local, State and National Grants for Gardens and the Environment

In some major cities there are Foundation Centers. Foundation Centers' focus is grant and funding sources. You can research under nutrition, health and wellness, and environment, and find grants that are available to you as an individual to do a project or you can work with an organization.

Associations and Leagues

Not to be discounted are Plant and Garden Associations and Junior Leagues

Garden Clubs

Garden Clubs are wonderful organizations. They host competitions and presentations by people learned in the field, some of whom contribute to the club in order to further research on a particular environmental topic or to have more people exposed to the specialized area that you have chosen to pursue work in.

## Local Businesses

Local businesses can be very important to you as a garden educator. Procurement of in-kind donations of plants from local nurseries, re-use centers have equipment and tools that could be of great use.

## CrowdFunding

The new way to get your project funded. Previously patronized by artists, filmmakers and musicians. Crowdfunding is a group of individuals who get together to fund your project. Being well-versed in Facebook and other social sites is vital as those who are investing in you exist in this virtual world. In order to get a project funded you must be precise and have all your paperwork together, but

nothing helps your pitch better than a great (authentic)

story.

## Chapter 7 – Getting Out There! Bringing Your Love of Nature to the World

In order to establish yourself as an expert in your field there are a number of things you can do that will get you involved with your community.

### Join an Association

It's important to familiarize yourself with local, state and national organizations that can help with exposure, support from members and access to individuals devoted to plants, gardens and the environment.

### The Chamber of Commerce

The job of the Chamber of Commerce is to promote local businesses and their services. Why not let them know about your contracting services at one of their regular meetings.

### Memberships

Memberships to specific clubs and organizations are perfect for connecting with important and skilled leaders in your chosen field. Being a member of the local or national Dahlia Society or outdoor club will open up a world of possibilities for learning and sharing.

## Volunteerism

Volunteering is one for the best ways to make an impact within a community. Helping others without any thought of receiving anything back can be addictive. Current research shows that more time spent in nature offers health benefits of stress release and lowering of blood pressure and giving is a key to lasting and genuine happiness.

## Offer to Teach a Workshop

Teaching a workshop will educate the public about who you are, what you do and the services you can provide. Why not host a workshop at the local community garden about composting food scraps for your garden? Or why not talk about the hard working worm and how his castings are considered "Black Gold?"

## **Parks and Recreation Centers**

Park and Recreation Centers are an amazing hubbub of activity, particularly during spring and summer. Often the centers are filled with youth who are participating in programming offered by a staff member. But, sometimes independent contractors are hired to teach their specialty to others. Dance teachers, cooking instructors, even community members who specialize in crafts or knitting are able to offer their services for a fee. It would be good to check with your local Park and Recreation Center about types of programming they offer during the year and ask if they would be interested in your services as a garden/environmental educator. Park and Recreations Centers and even Early Child Development Centers can benefit from special "Guests" willing to bring nature to their door.

*Head Start, Early Child Developments, Daycares?

Daycares were a focal point on my route when I worked on the bookmobile with the public library. These communities of tiny learners often are site-based and may not leave the premises to be in touch with it.

## Chapter 8 – What's Next? Readying to work with your Funders and Organizations

### Working as an Independent Contractor

The type of work you do is very vital. Connecting individuals with the natural world is one way of ensuring appreciation and stewardship of the land for the present and future to come. As an independent contractor, you are free to take on a variety of projects. You want to be aware of several important factors in choosing projects.

- What is the timeline for your chosen project? (How much planning, meetings, grant writing or physical labor is involved?)

- Length or duration of a project. (Will this be a project that lasts a few weeks, months or longer?)

- What are your time considerations or constraints? (What time would your organization or individual want you to start?

Are mornings the best time to get started with your work? Would afternoons or early evenings be more appropriate for working clients? Will you be in a clinic or hospital as timing is key when dealing with clients' medication times? Schools are open in the early mornings, so are you an early morning person?)

- Insurance: Personal Liability Insurance is important to have so that you are mindful of accidents that could occur or work that might not meet the expectations of your client.

- A working contract that is geared toward your particular gardening niche will help potential clients to respect your work and get you paid. It would be important to get a lawyer to look over your contract.

## Working With Your Chosen Organization

You have found your chosen organization and you have been working on negotiations. You have either found a grant that is suitable or your organization has available funding, now it is time to get to work! This is the exciting part of your job. If you have the opportunity to put your special spin on your green niche participation then now is the time to do it! Working with an organization has an upside and downside. The upside is that you already have a support system in place. You have key administrative individuals who want to see the (your) project come to reality and often co-workers for the agency will be able to volunteer some time or services to help get that raised bed garden built or that shady bench seat for seniors built that overlooks the serenity garden. The downside could be red tape and miscommunication between yourself and those in charge of getting you paid by the granting institution or the private funders. These are a couple of things that could happen that are not positive but can be overcome. Don't give up hope! Make sure that you and your organization are on the same page concerning your work, hours, and when your payment is due, who you will have assisting you if that is what you need and who the point people are.

Frequent checks and balances are mandatory if you want to

keep good communication.

## The Granting Process

Being awarded a grant could be as simple as the results

of filling out a one page document with a small group of

private donors, or it could be as complex as several

hundred pages which encompasses a variety of contributing

organizations. Some grants may be received by you very

timely and you are able to go ahead and get started on your

work, while other grants may go through so many levels of

red tape that it could be months or even a year before the

grant monies become available. You due diligence is very

important here. If the granting process involves you in a

substantial way then you must be on time with providing

the appropriate information to your chosen organization.

They will need a detailed projection of what your project will be, where it will take place, what it will cost and who will be involved.

## Contracts with Non-Profits or Individuals

A contract with a non-profit organization could be very rewarding. You might be creating a healing fruit and vegetable garden for low-income, young mothers and then creating nutrition based garden activities that work in harmony within the garden. A garden for a homeless population will serve the needs of those individuals as well as the community. Working with non-profits give you a chance to work with your community and often a needy community. Working with individuals differs in that you might work with one person or a small group of three to five. There are normally less people to check-in with for decisions about your work and often you can make flexible arrangements with work times.

## Learning Grant Writing for Yourself

Have you ever considered becoming a grant writer? Grant writing can be extremely profitable to yourself as well as any organization looking to create or retain healthful and innovative programming for its clients. If you know how to garner money for a potential organization, you will become a star! Being a grant writer is not for everyone, and filling out hundreds of very detailed documents and spreadsheets and narratives may be too cerebral for your taste. But if you are interested in the craft of grant writing and locating, and you create a winning grant response, then you can add that as part of your Green Niche business services for which you can charge accordingly. Online adult colleges have grant writing courses for a small fee.

I was able to work with a "Friends of the Library Branch" group. I created a series of workshops that showed days and times and what my expectations would be. I would be working with a group of after school students. I would need $500 for the brief project for my services and a small set of supplies for some of the gardening activities. The Children's librarian gave me a short one page application for the amount I would need for the project and it just so happened that the head of the group was a garden enthusiast who invited me to his home to view his own garden, which was lovely. I filled out the application along with my projected activities, and within two weeks I was issued a check for my program and services!

## Meetings

You will encounter many meetings along the way to your project getting off the ground. You new Green Niche business will require you to be highly visible and to be very accountable for your potential projects and ideas. People want to know whom they are getting involved with, and this can mean meetings after work hours with community members or individuals. Be prepared to talk up your

business and reassure your public that your services would
be a perfect fit for their project. Your love and commitment
to the Natural World and…

## Chapter 9 – Digging In and Getting To Work!

### Implementation

Implementation of your project will be one of the most rewarding activities you will carry out. Once you are able to set up your workshops or your garden program, you can really see your diligent work come to fruition. No project comes away totally without a hitch, but if you have implemented the suggestions I have set forth in Chapters 1 through 8 then you are well on your way.

### Safety

Safety is number one! You will need to be aware of where to store tools and how to keep yourself as well as any volunteers safe while working with any sharp or heavy garden equipment. You should also be familiar with the equipment you will be using so that you can educate others on it's uses and safety. Make an estimate of what you will be needing and be sure to check with your organization or group about keeping themselves safe while on the work site.

## Volunteers and Work Days

As mentioned in the paragraph above, safety is of the utmost importance when working in natural areas and especially when you work with non-paid volunteers. As volunteers are not covered by their own liability insurance, you will want to make sure that they will not be exposed to too many risky situations. Educating about tool usage and worksite safety will remedy many potential hazards. What is a Work Day? A Work Day is a day that is set aside by yourself and the group that you are working with. On this day you and your volunteers can be encouraged and help get large amounts of work done. Need that huge mound of mulch or dirt distributed throughout the worksite? The Work Day will provide you with ample and willing volunteers who have been cleared by the appropriate group leaders. You can often provide beverages and in-kind donations are of pizza or sandwiches are sometimes possible to negotiate with nearby restaurants or cafes.

## Photo and Financial Documentation

Photo documentation is part of the backbone for your culminating project. In addition to your paper documentation, photos also help to chronicle results, the 'before and after.' It will also be very helpful in securing future contracts of the same or smaller size. Paper documentation which dictates your initial ideas of your project to the culminating activity is important to document and keep all along the way, having photo and paper documentation will assist in showing your next potential client the written and the visuals of what you do. Please keep a log of your activities from the beginning of your project until the end. Then convert them into a professional portfolio or PowerPoint presentation for your Green Niche business.

## Project Completion!

Your project is done! You have accomplished so much by this point. Now that your project is complete you must do a follow up assessment. You also have been able to become involved in the environmental connection of your community members and private individuals. If you were not the grant writer you participated heartily in the planning and organization of the whole project. Take a moment to appreciate all the hard work you have done and the new connections you have made. Following up with your chosen group or individual will hopefully help you to become even closer to your core reasons for working to connect people with nature. The hope is that you have made friendships for life and have great references that will validate all your hard work and community involvement. Congratulations! Now, on to your next exciting project.